[Life 101]

» an illustrated guide

**Andrews McMeel
Publishing, LLC**

Kansas City

[Life 101]

» an illustrated guide

» Geoffrey Day-Lewis

#1 [Be yourself.]

#2 [Don't blow with the wind]

#3 [Try to be positive.]

#4

[Have regular check-ups.]

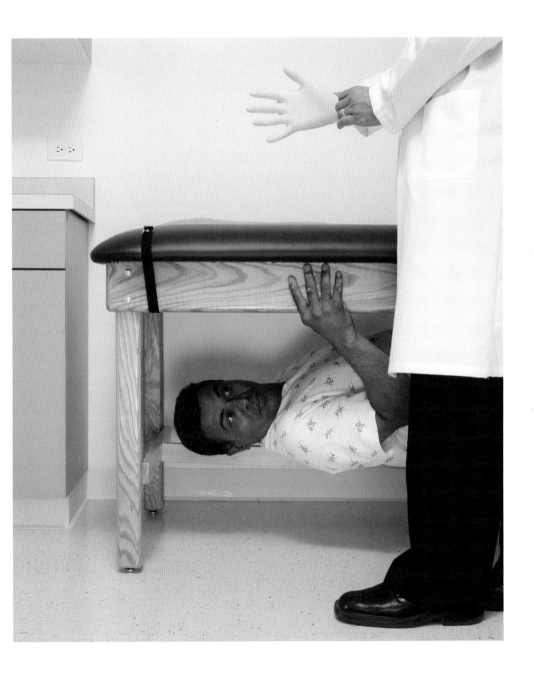

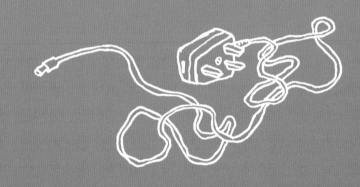

#5 [Embrace technology.]

#6 [Never be too proud to ask for help.]

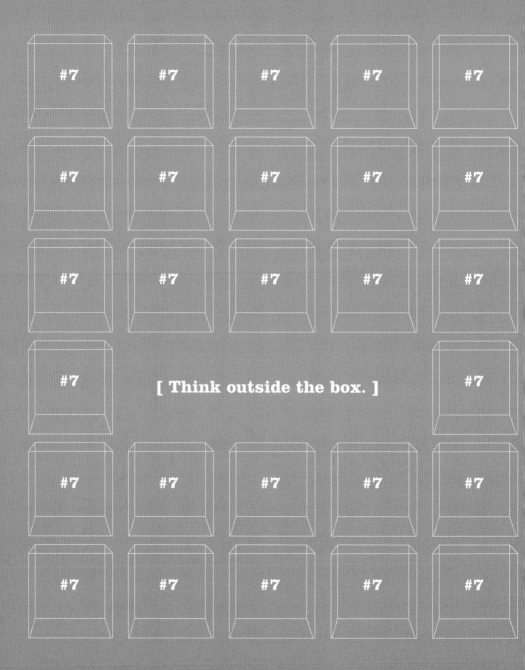

[Think outside the box.]

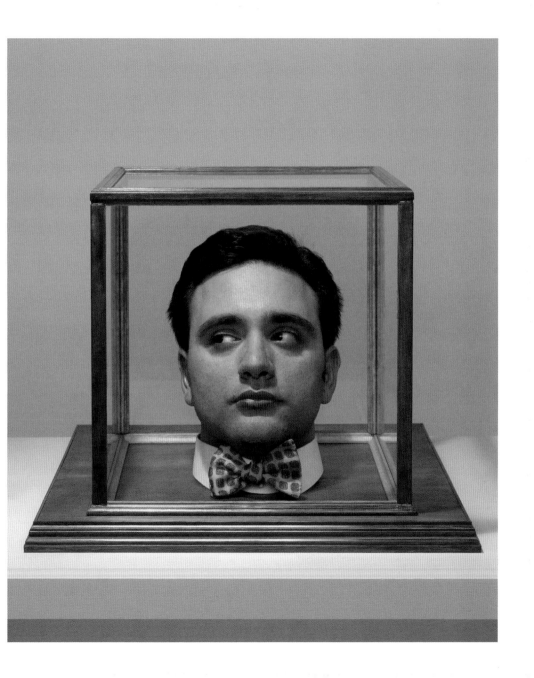

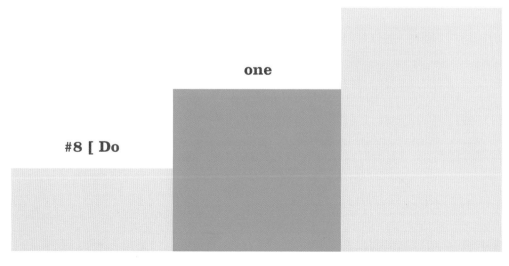

#8 [Do

one

thing

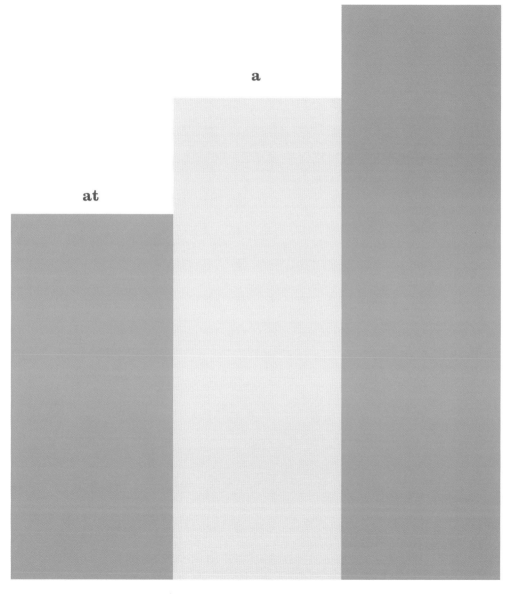

#9 [Life isn't always fair.]

#10 [Sometimes it takes just one good idea.]

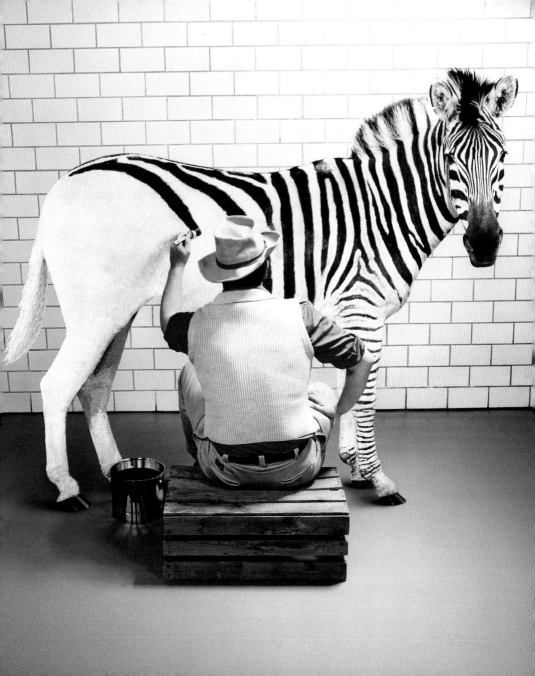

#11 [Always try to make a good impression.]

#12 [If you can't say something nice . . .

then don't say anything at all.]

#13 [Learn to share.]

#14 [Keep your family close.]

#15 [Choose your housemates carefully.]

#16 [Be gentle with the earth.]

#17 [Keep an open mind.]

#18 [Beauty is all around you.]

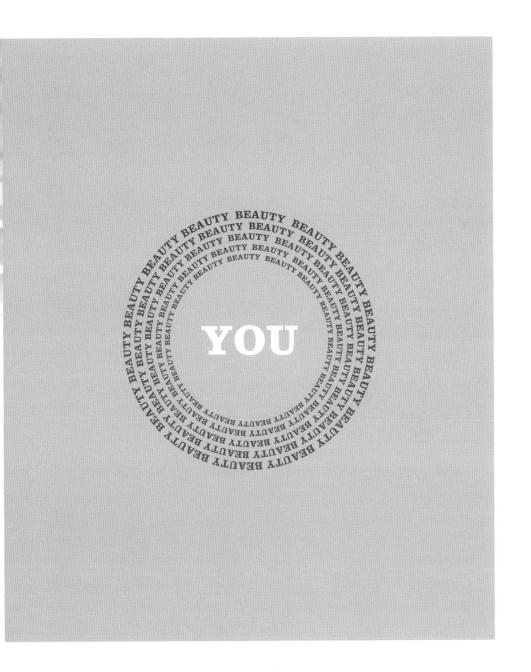

#19 [Seek and you shall find.]

#20 [Preparation is the key to success.]

#21 [Don't hide your light under a bushel.]

#22 [Don't be envious.]

#23 [Take time to read books.]

#24 [Grow old gracefully.]

#25 [Good posture is important.]

#26 [Eat your greens.]

#27 [Don't be afraid to speak up.]

#28 [Never **rupt** inter when

you are being flattered.]

#29 [Plan ahead.]

#30 [Don't get carried away.]

#31 [You can if you think you can.]

#32 [If at first you don't succeed, try, try, and try again.]

#33

remember compliments

#34 [Believe in love at first sight.]

#35 [Be a good listener.]

· NORTH POLE ·
POLICE DEPARTMENT

CLAUS, SANTA :
SK53074116802

#36 [Respect your elders.]

#37, #38, #39, #40, #41, #42, #43, #44, #45, #46,
#47, #48, #49, #50, #51, #52, #53, #54, #55, #56,
#57, #58, #59, #60, #61, #62, #63, #64, #65,
#66, #67, #68, #69

#70 [Exercise regularly.]

#71 [The key to life is balance.]

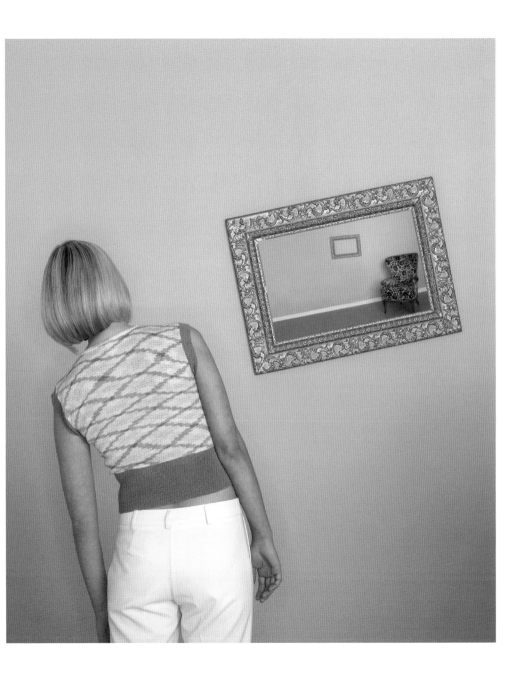

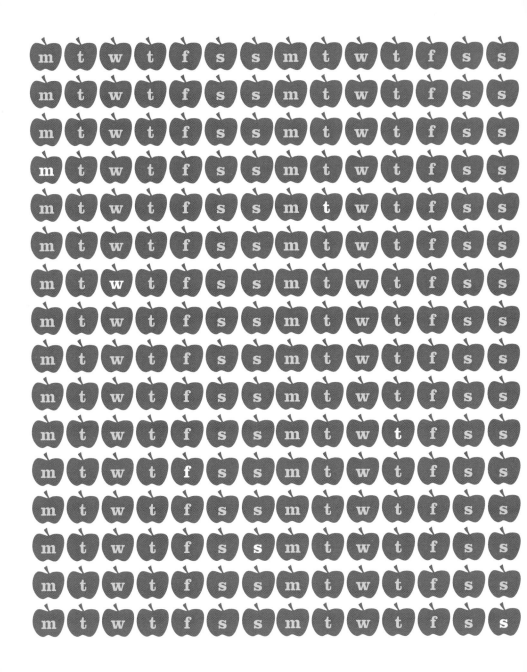

#72 [An apple a day keeps the doctor away.]

#73 [Healthy body, healthy mind.]

#74 [Remember to . . .

stretch.]

#75 [Take an interest in the arts.]

#76 [Don't lose your head.]

#77 [Get plenty of fresh air.]

#78 [Stay in touch with your friends.]

#79 [Be a team player.]

#80 [Remember to dance.]

#81 [Try to travel.]

#82 [Look both ways

[before crossing the street.]

#83 [Expect the unexpected.]

#85 [Honesty is the best policy.]

#86 [Sometimes you need to let your feet do the talking.

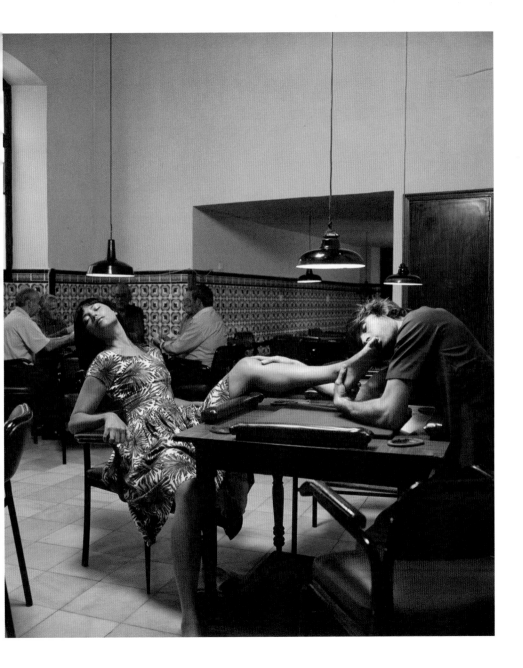

#87 [It is better to give than receive.]

#88 [Do one good deed every day.]

#89 [Love thy neighbor.]

#90 [Cleanliness is next to godliness.]

#91 [Take time out for yourself.]

#92 [Be observant.]

#93 [Patience is a virtue, possess it if you can.]

#94 [Mind your own business.]

#95 [Be a communicator.]

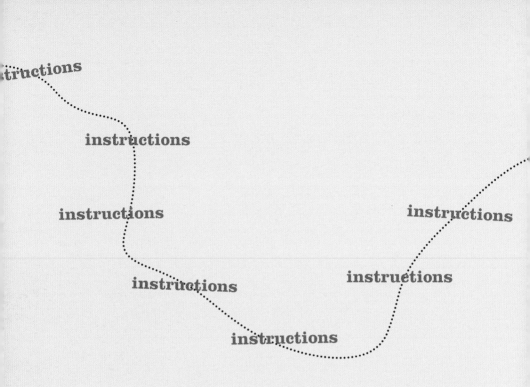

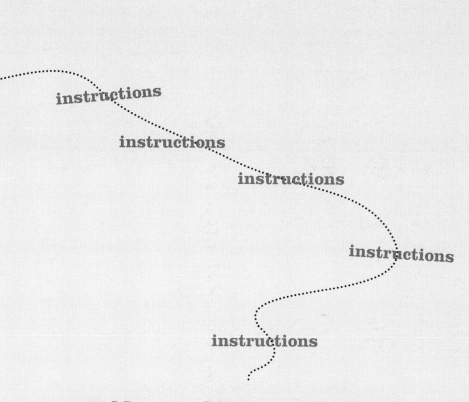

#96 [Learn to follow instructions.]

#97 [Wear sunscreen.]

#98 [Keep your feet on the ground.]

#99 [Always give it your best shot.]

#100

[Get a good night's sleep.]

#101 [Above all, just be yourself.]